RV LIVING

A Beginner's Guide To Turning Your Motorhome Dream Into Reality

© **Copyright 2020 by Bill Oatfield – All rights reserved.**

In no way is it legal to reproduce, duplicate, or transmit any part of this document in either electronic means or in printed format. Recording of this publication is strictly prohibited and any storage of this document is not allowed unless with written permission from the publisher.

The information provided herein is stated to be truthful and consistent, in that any liability, in terms of inattention or otherwise, by any usage or abuse of any policies, processes, or directions contained within is the solitary and utter responsibility of the recipient reader. Under no circumstances will any legal responsibility or blame be held against the author for any reparation, damages, or monetary loss due to the information herein, either directly or indirectly.

The information herein is offered for informational purposes solely, and is universal as so. The presentation of the information is without contract or any type of guarantee assurance.

Legal Disclaimer: all photos used in this book are published on Flickr.com under the Attribution 2.0 Generic (CC BY 2.0) license.

ERRORS

Please contact us if you find any errors.

We have taken every effort to ensure the quality and correctness of this book. However, after going over the book draft time and again, we sometimes don't see the forest for the trees anymore.

If you notice any errors, we would really appreciate it if you could contact us directly before taking any other action. This allows us to quickly fix it.

Errors: errors@semsoli.com

REVIEWS

Reviews and feedback help improve this book and the author.

If you enjoy this book, we would greatly appreciate it if you were able to take a few moments to share your opinion and post a review online.

ENQUIRIES & FEEDBACK

For any general feedback about the book, please feel free to contact me at this email address: contact@semsoli.com

Table of Contents

Introduction..8

1. Choosing The Right RV For You...................10
    Class A
    Class B
    Class C

2. New Or Used? That's The Question...............18
    Deciding on Buying a New or Used Rv
    Dealerships
    RV Shows

3. What To Look For When Checking Out An RV 24
    Why You Need to Test the Systems of an RV
    Water System
    Electrical System
    Propane System
    Other Things to Check
    Get Roadside Assistance

4. How To Finance The Purchase Of An RV.....34
    Be Prepared to Haggle
    How to Get a Loan
    Know Your Credit Score
    Mistakes to Avoid When Getting a Loan

5. Preparing For RV Living 40
    Choosing a Domicile State
    How to Get a Permanent Address
    Set up Electronic Deliveries
    Set up a Digital Signature
    Use the Campsite Address
    Use the Local Post Office Address
    Voting
    Medical Care
    Jury Duty

6. How To Budget For The Road 52
    Budget: Where to Start?
    How to Save Money
    Finding a Job on the Road
    Finding an Online Source of Income
    Blogging
    Selling on Amazon
    Drop shipping
    Teaching English
    Freelancing

7. Getting Along In An RV 64
    Make Sure Your RV Has Enough Room
    Choose a Sturdy RV
    Assign Roles
    Respect Each Other's Storage Space
    Assign a Place For Your Pet
    Avoid Clutter

Do Not Travel Too Much in One Day
Stick to Your Budget
Communicate Openly

8. Finding The Best Campgrounds, Paid Or Not..72
What is Boondocking
Apps for Boondocking
Campground Sites Memberships

9. RV Resources..................................80
RV Lifestyle Websites
RV Lifestyle Apps
Finding Campsites Websites
Making Money Online Websites
Memberships Websites
Roadside Assistance Websites

Final Words...84

BONUS CHAPTER: What Are Shipping Container Homes?...86

Did You Like This Book?........................94

About The Author................................95

Introduction

Thank you for purchasing this book, *'RV Living: A Beginner's Guide To Turning Your Motorhome Dream Into Reality'*. Clearly, you have an interest in understanding what truly goes into living full-time, or even part-time, in a motorhome.

And you have come to the right place!

It was Mark Twain who said:

"Twenty years from now you will be more disappointed by the things that you didn't do than by the ones you did do. So throw off the bowlines. Sail away from the safe harbor. Catch the trade winds in your sails. Explore. Dream. Discover."

With choosing to live in a recreational vehicle, or RV, you are doing exactly that.

RV living is essentially living in a recreational vehicle full-time, like you would in an apartment or a house. The most common recreational vehicle many think of is an RV camper, which houses all of the amenities of home within the confines of a bus. Many RV campers come with lavish looks on the inside as well as pertinent designs on the outside, but a lot of those will cost a good deal of cash up front. This book will address the many ways in which you can purchase an RV, as well as how to get the best bang for your buck when it comes to the quality of your potential RV camper.

This book covers all facets of RV living, from how to cope with living in close proximity to your loved ones all the way to handling your mail and doctors appointments. This comprehensive book on RV living will teach you how to budget your money, make money while on the road, cover extra expenses and accessories that come with RV living, as well as guide you through the process of choosing the perfect recreational vehicle for you and your loved ones.

However, RV living is not just comprised of purchasing a vehicle and coming up with a budget. There are also other facets to navigate, like residing in such close proximity with other adults and possibly even pets, how to save money on the road, and how to work (if necessary) while you are traveling. All of these things come into question at some point in time whenever someone is traveling full-time in an RV, and they are legitimate questions that will be answered within the walls of this book.

When you finish this book, not only will you know if living in a recreational vehicle is something you wish to do, but you will have all of the basics at your disposal so you can navigate this new and adventurous lifestyle with ease and confidence.

Now is the day on which you can take the **first step** to **changing your life**.

Thank you for purchasing this book, and I hope you find it to be the best resource you could possibly have on RV living.

Welcome to the RV family!

1. Choosing The Right RV For You

"I got it one piece at a time
And it didn't cost me a dime
You'll know it's me when I come through your town
I'm gonna ride around in style
I'm gonna drive everybody wild
'Cause I'll have the only one there is around"

One Piece At A Time – Johnny Cash

<u>Key Takeaway</u>: *There are three classes of RVs: A, B, and C. Each have their own upsides and downsides, but the most popular class for many beginning full-time RV residents is Class C.*

When a living space and an engine are combined into one vehicle, it is called a motorhome. The more common phrase is "RV," and it is designated today as a permanent living space for many individuals. No matter the type of motorhome you wish to choose for your particular situation, they all fall into three different classes: A, B, and C.

***

Class A

Class As are the largest motorhomes, with lengths and widths up to that of a tour bus. If you picture a Greyhound bus, you have an idea of how large one of these things is.

Example of a Class A RV

Many relish over these RVs because of the space inside as well as the amenities at their disposal. These motorhomes usually have lavish decorations inside to make the interior space seem more like a traditional house, but as the amenities and interior beauty escalate, so does the price. Some used ones can be found for as cheap as $60,000, while many that are outfitted and brand new can cost someone up to millions of dollars, depending on how they wish to outfit it.

Class A motorhomes can be up to 45 feet long, which give the RV dwellers ample room, and part of that space is usually used for a master suite as well as a full-sized bathroom and shower. Some can come preinstalled with their own washer and dryer unit, and come decked out with multiple sliders that can expand the width of the bus by 14-feet. It is the most customizable motorhome with some of the add-ons being an ice machine, a flat-screen television, and a dishwasher, not to mention all of the storage space that comes with it.

However, everything has a downside, and Class A motorhomes are no different. Fuel economy is slim-to-none with a vehicle like this, with the average gas mileage being somewhere between 9-12 miles per gallon. Another downside to a motorhome like this is the necessity for a toad, which is a separate vehicle that comes along with the travel. When you set up camp in something as big as this, it becomes impractical to constantly pack it up and drive every time someone needs to run into town for an appointment or food. This means maintaining two vehicles that are constantly on the road.

***

Class B

Then there are the Class B motorhomes, which are simply campervans.

Example of a Class B RV

This is the smallest motorhome class, but many people have been known to outfit them with lavish interiors, making them incredibly comfortable and livable. For an individual who wants to travel a great deal with their RV, this is the most affordable option. The price ranges from $40,000 to $80,000 while still coming with all of the basic amenities a living situation needs: a bed area, a sink, a stove top, and a refrigerator.

They do still have some storage, though not nearly as much as the other two classes, and are most popular among single individuals who do not understand how to work a tow hitch.

The size variance is the greatest on a Class B motorhome. They lack the over-cab portion that a Class C motorhome provides (see below), but the utilization of a cargo van base means the size can range from a standard full-sized cargo van all the way to a 20-foot vehicle.

Some of the plus sides to this type of RV are the gas mileage (18-20 miles per gallon!), the ease of maneuverability, and the fact that many standard Class B motorhomes can fit into a standard garage and a mall parking space.

However, this class does have drastic downsides: there is no master suite, so the bed is usually a drop-down table or a fold-out couch. There is also not much space, so maneuvering within the motorhome will be difficult. And the entertainment afforded to someone utilizing the space within this class of motorhome is either a radio or a small-screen television.

***

Class C

Class Cs are what many consider "typical motorhomes." They have a normal chassis (the base frame for the motor vehicle) and a bunking situation above the cab.

Example of a Class C RV

Their length ranges anywhere between 20 and 33 feet, and the front looks like a normal van or pickup truck, with the RV's body extending over the cab where the driver and passenger dwell during travel. This extended space above the cab is the sleeping space, and this area can easily fit a queen or king-sized bed, making it very comfortable for two individuals. They are much smaller than a Class A motorhome, but they do not lack in space. What it loses in elongated space it makes up for in interior compartments.

Space in a Class C is also utilized better, with many storage compartments on the outside to store things such as portable grills, televisions, and sewer hoses. Plus, with the smaller length of the motorhome, it is much easier to maneuver down the road and in motorhome parks. This class of motorhome can have a price tag of anywhere between $45,000 to $140,000.

Another upside to going with a Class C motorhome is the fact that a service and warranty work is easier to come by. Because the driving portion of the motorhome usually has a brand name cab and a drive train, many auto dealers cannot turn around and claim ignorance on how to service the vehicle. Plus, with the diminished size from a Class A motorhome, many more camping ground opportunities become available for you to utilize. The gas mileage is a bit better compared to a Class A, but you will still only get around 15 miles to the gallon in a Class C motorhome.

Yet, as with everything else, there are downsides: there aren't many slide out options for a Class C motorhome, so expanding the width of the RV is not an option. Plus, when your RV needs to have maintenance work performed on it, if you aren't attempting to do it yourself, then you will end up losing your entire home for the duration of the service time. However, the same is true for the RVs in the other two classes.

***

Now you know the differences between a Class A, B and C RV motorhome.

For most people, a Class C RV would be the best option. If you are on a budget, and don't mind getting cozy in a small space a lot, you may want to consider a Class B Rv.

And if price isn't an issue, and you are comfortable riding a vehicle the size of a bus, then a Class A RV is your go-to motorhome!

Once you have decided which class best fits your needs and wants, the following pressing question arises: should you buy a new or used RV?

That is what we will cover next.

2. New Or Used? That's The Question

"I see my path, but I don't know where it leads. Not knowing where I'm going is what inspires me to travel it."

Rosalia de Castro

Key Takeaway: *Purchasing an RV can be an intimidating process for a first-timer. The more you learn about RVs prior to any purchase decision, the better. You will better understand your own likes and dislikes, you will know what to avoid, and you will be able to leverage your expertise when negotiating price. Start with reading up on RVs. And then get your feet wet by visiting local dealerships and possibly an RV show. You are not going to know what coffee tastes like if you only read books about it, right? It is the same with getting a feel for RVs.*

What is most intimidating for many first-time (potential) RV owners is the actual purchasing process. Many don't know whether to go new or used, whether to pay cash or finance, and many do not understand the basic elements to look at before committing to purchasing an RV.

The short version is:

- Buy a new RV, and your main concern is going to be how to finance it.
- Buy a used RV, and your main concern is going to be not buying a pig in a poke.

In any case, you can save yourself a lot of future headaches if you make an informed decision now. The more you educate yourself about RVs beforehand, the better you will know what you want and expect from an RV, and what you will need to look out for.

***

Deciding on Buying a New or Used Rv

To get an idea what to look for when buying an RV, the best thing to do is to take a look at a couple of RVs first, and pick an expert's brain. Sure, you can learn a lot from books like this or watching explainer videos online. But that is not enough. You will only get a real feel for what to look for when buying an RV if you have seen and touched a bunch. In person.

Just like purchasing a regular car, you will always get a better deal buying from an individual than from a dealership. However, first-time buyers would benefit from a trip to a dealership, if only to pick the salesman's brain about the vehicle as a whole. Remember, we are not buying yet. We are simply orienting ourselves on what is on the market.

So where do you go to when you want to take a look at the various RVs on the market?

These are your two best options:

- Local Dealerships
- RV Shows

Make sure you have a decent understanding of RVs before your visit, so you know the right questions to ask! Read this book, and check out websites and Youtube videos on RV living. After you have done that, you can be confident that you have a solid level of knowledge, decent enough to make a visit to a local dealer or RV show worthwhile.

***

Dealerships

There are a ton of RV dealers out there. Unless you are living in a very remote area, you will definitely be able to find a local RV dealer.

These dealers have a great variety of motorhomes at display. Like car salesmen, they get paid commission on their sales. But no one expects you to buy an RV on the spot at your first visit. Regardless of the class you are interested in, purchasing an RV is a big financial investment. A wise (wo)man will first want to do due diligence before committing to such a purchase. And RV dealers understand this. If you do feel pressured into making a purchase decision on the spot, take a breath and keep your guard up. This is your money we are talking about. Spend it wisely, and only after enough deliberation.

With that said, feel free to take a look at their showroom, and pick the brains of the person that is showing you around. Take notes on anything that catches your attention. You may want to do further research when you come home. And do not forget to bring your camera and take a lot of pictures!

***

RV Shows

Attending an RV show is another excellent way of checking out the many different motorhomes that are on offer. These are big events, with performances, live music and of course many RVs at display. Check out the calendar of the Recreational Vehicle Industry Association (RVIA), rvia.org, to find one near you. Most shows are organized in spring, summer and fall.

There will be many more motorhomes that you can check out at an RV show, compared to visiting a dealership. Also, a dealership often has an exclusive relationship with a particular brand. This means that you will only be able to see RVs from a particular brand at that particular dealership. Finally, you will find representatives of both dealers and manufacturers at RV shows. So if one person cannot answer your question, you can just walk to the next booth and ask it to someone else!

The downside of an RV show is that you cannot visit them year round. Unless you want to book a flight ticket, you will have to wait until an RV show is organized in a city near you. It would be best to first visit a dealership, and then attend an RV show later on.

Keep in mind that RV shows are also full of salesmen, looking to close a deal. Like when visiting a dealership, make sure you have your wits about you. Before you even walk into the venue, decide whether you are willing to buy an RV today or not. Stick to that decision, no matter what! Keep in mind that your main reason for being at this show is to learn more about the different types of RVs on the market. This knowledge will help you to make a more informed decision later on. Plus, you will be able to leverage your expertise when negotiating price.

***

That is how you can get an idea of the different types of RVs that are on the market, so you can make an informed decision on what you want, and whether to buy a new or used RV.

Next up, we'll discuss what to look for when testing an RV, so you can buy the best RV for you.

3. What To Look For When Checking Out An RV

"Brrrm brm brm brm brm brm brrrm
Brrrm brm brm brm brm brm brrrm

Take me riding in the car, car
Take me riding in the car, car"

Riding in my Car – Woody Guthrie

<u>Key Takeaway</u>: *Testing an RV's systems is the most important thing you will need to do prior to purchasing it. This is why it is crucial you first educate yourself on RVs. If you do not feel comfortable testing the systems of the vehicle you are interested in on your own, hire an expert. The main systems you will need to check are the water, electrical and propane systems.*

The biggest piece of advice is to never purchase an RV without testing every single system first.

In this chapter, you will learn why this is so important, and which systems you will need to test.

***

Why You Need to Test the Systems of an RV

You have to make sure that every single system works and has been maintenanced the way it needs to be. Whether you are purchasing new or used, making sure all of the systems are tested is necessary. The last thing you want to be stuck with is an RV whose systems begin to break down one week into your new journey.

If you want to check these systems yourself, you will need a:

- Water hose
- Charged car battery
- Cigarette lighter power adapter
- Charger to plug into that adapter
- Normal wall outlet adapter
- Regular propane cylinder, and a
- Truck with a towing package (only if you are looking at a motorhome that tows behind your vehicle)

If you are uncomfortable with testing the systems yourself, it is wise to bring in someone to test them for you. This will cost you around $180 to $300. However, if things are found wrong with the RV before negotiations begin taking place, that can be used as a real bargaining chip when agreeing on price. Not to mention the money you keep in your pocket if you decide to call the whole thing off.

How do you test the systems? This process is not as overwhelming as it feels if you take it one step at a time. Purchasing an RV does not happen in a day, and if you span the process over the course of even a week, you will feel much better about your purchase over all.

***

Water System

In order to test the water system, you need to hook the hose you brought with you up to the water intake line of the RV and then hook the other one up to some sort of running water outside the RV. This is what it means to be "hooked up," but some people refer to it as being on "city water."

Once this hookup is complete and you have determined that water is flowing into the RV, then begin turning on faucets, shower heads, and flushing the toilet. Make sure all of these things flow efficiently and disperse water the way they should. In order to gauge the water pressure, turn the outside spigot on before hooking up the hose. Whatever that water pressure is, should be the water pressure for the inside of the RV.

Then, leave the water running slowly out of one of the faucets, then shut everything else down. Go outside and find the sewer outlet, and while you are bending over to find it, check underneath the RV. Make sure there are no leaks or spillage of any sort. Then, as a check, drain the water from the RV to make sure there is no black water, or water that is dirtied or contaminated in any way from the RV. Keep in mind throughout the draining process to make sure there is no leakage anywhere.

After this, one more water test remains: checking the water pump. To do this, you need to locate the RV's fresh water storage tank. Fill it with water and then remove the hose hookup from the "city water." Then, find the switch to turn on the water pump and listen to it. If there is a lot of noise or shaking (some noise will happen depending on the model, but it should not roar) it means the water pump will need to be replaced soon, and that can be used as another bargaining chip when coming to a reasonable price-point. But, when you have the water pump turned on, try the faucets yet again and check the water pressure that is instituted by the water pump. Then, go back outside and check for leaks near the water pump. If you can get through with no issues and leaks, then your water system in the RV is ready to go!

***

Electrical System

Then, there is the electrical system to test. Most RVs run directly off a 12-volt battery, which is the equivalent of a car or marine battery. But, they also (usually) have the capability to plug into a 30-amp or 50-amp system at an RV park. For both of these power sources, there will be two separate breakers. The 12-volt battery controls most of the internal indicators and lights, as well as the refrigerator unit in the RV. Everything else usually runs off the hook up at the RV park you dock at.

For testing the 12-volt system, connect a good battery to the RV and begin turning on internal RV lights and indicators. Make sure they work. Plug in the cigarette charger adaptor and plug something in. Make sure that works as well. If they are not working, the first thing to do is to check the fuses in the fusebox, then check to make sure the battery you are using has enough juice in it.

Once you can make sure all of this is good to go, then plug the RV's external power cable into a source of electricity. Most RVs have a plug that is a three-prong setup, so if you want to connect it to a basic wall outlet you might need an adaptor. Make sure the breaker in the box is turned on, and then check to make sure the rest of the internal appliances work properly. Plug a phone charger directly into a wall outlet in the RV and see if it will charge the phone, and remember to check the lights again in the RV. They should work no matter what power source the vehicle is hooked up to. Again, if nothing is working, check the breaker box to make sure no switches have been flipped. But, if everything works, then this system test is done as well!

***

Propane System

Then, testing the propane system is next. This is the final major component of the RV's system, and this is what fuels the stovetop, any additional heaters, the refrigerator's backup system, and the hot water heater. In order to test this, find where the propane cylinders are and switch it out for the one you brought. Propane lines screw left for tightness and right for looseness, which is the opposite of everything else. Once you have the line connected to your filled propane cylinder, twist the nozzle on top of your cylinder. When you hear the short hiss, the propane will begin to fill the lines of the RV.

Then, the testing begins. Go into the RV and turn on a burner, then light a match. If the propane is making it through the lines, the propane should catch the match, therefore heating the burner just as any home gas stove would. Make sure to test all of the stovetop burners in this fashion.

For the oven, there is usually a pilot light that needs to be lit in order to test it. But, the test for the oven is the same way for the stoves.

Once you have those tested, go outside and unplug your outer power cable. Then, look at the control panel on the refrigerator. Find the "auto" setting if there is one, and if not, then look for the "gas" and "lp" toggle on it. Either way, flip it to make sure the refrigerator is now running off the propane source. Listen closely. If you hear any sort of clicking sound that extends for a long period of time or any sort of "check" light clicks itself on, then you have an issue with the backup system to the refrigerator. But, if you do not, stick around until you feel some sort of elemental change inside the refrigerator.

Then, it's off to the water heater tank. Follow the individual instructions to light it and get it going, and then go inside and turn on a hot water faucet. Wait until there is hot water coming out.

Once you have verified that all of these components are working properly and have been tested, then the RV has no issues with its major systems! Keep in mind, you still have to get the RV inspected, but this means the RV is good for purchase if you don't wish to inherit any issues.

***

Other Things to Check

Other things to keep in mind that enhance living in a recreational vehicle are things like cable hookups in order to test the television and cable outlet and built-in radios and DVD players that will need to be tested as well. However, in all of the testing of the "fun things," do not forget to test the RV's more important features, like the frame and roof. Make sure things are solid, free of damage, and unwavering. For the roof, a typical RV should be able to support one solid person with no issues of bending or wavering. If the roof is squishy or soggy, that is a massive issue to deal with.

Also, give the tires a good kick. Check the brakes and the fluids in the vehicle, and ask the seller how long the vehicle has been sitting. When checking the brakes, listen out for a noise inside of the tires. This indicates that the electrical brakes are working the way they should. If you do not hear that sound, address it immediately. Also, check the axles and make sure no major damage has been issued to them. Make sure the motorhome is sitting level, both front to back and side to side, when sitting stationary on level ground. If all of this seems intimidating, many garages will have someone that will accompany you to look over the RV at an hourly rate (which spans anywhere between $25-$75 an hour).

Testing the systems yourself before bringing in an inspector is imperative. While inspectors will give it an overall look, their job is not to test every facet of every system. Their job is to make sure nothing major is damaged so that you will be safe on the road.

This means checking the mechanisms under the hood, giving the engine a good look, testing the lights, checking the windshield wipers, and making sure nothing major is leaking. If the test is done to a car for inspection, it will be done to the RV. However, that leaves a lot to be desired. The inspection is required simply to prove to your insurance company insuring the vehicle that it is approved to run safely on the road.

That does not mean its system will be in tip-top shape.

***

Get Roadside Assistance

Finally, please understand: no matter what RV you choose to buy, and no matter if you choose new or used, always have dependable roadside assistance. Always. Things will happen on the road when a vehicle like this is being run to its limits, and even though the vehicle is created to handle the rough and rugged terrain of many different types of environments, it means there are higher chances of something going wrong while on the road.

Why?

Because that is the environment the vehicle is living in! Just like there is a higher percentage of rust with cars in states that salt their roads heavily during the winter months, there is a higher percentage of something happening to your vehicle while on the road because that is the vehicle's dominant environment.

These are some of the companies that offer roadside assistance:

- Good Sam (Goodsamroadside.com)
- Coach-Net (Coach-Net.com)
- Progressive (Progressive.com)

Pay a little money upfront, and save yourself a lot of money and trouble later on!

***

If the RV passes all your main systems checks, you are no longer shooting in the dark. If you decide to go ahead with the purchase, you can be confident that this motorhome is going to give you years of pleasure on the road!

Buying an RV is not cheap though. If you are like most people, you will probably need to finance at least part of the purchase price. How you would go about financing the purchase of your dream RV is what you will learn in the following chapter.

4. How To Finance The Purchase Of An RV

"A budget tells us what we can't afford, but it doesn't keep us from buying it."

William Feather

Key Takeaway: Whether you are considering a new or used one, purchasing an RV motorhome requires a serious financial investment. Be prepared to haggle down the price. And if you are going to take out a loan, be smart about it. Know your credit score, shop around, and know what you can afford.

When buying an RV, your safest bet is a new one. It just rolled out of the factory and has never been used. Moreover, you can expect the latest and greatest in terms of design and motor parts.

High quality comes at a price though. How you are going to finance the purchase?

Because a new RV requires a bigger financial investment, the advice in this chapter is mostly tailored to this situation. However, most of it applies equally to purchasing a used RV.

***

Be Prepared to Haggle

First off, when financing an RV, keep in mind that many RV salesmen expect you to haggle on the price. Many RVs on the lots are marked up as much as 30% from the suggested retail price, so do not be intimidated to ask for a lower price than the ticket price on the vehicle.

***

How to Get a Loan

If financing is the way to go for you, there are some things to keep in mind: try to find someone outside the dealership that will loan you the money. RV dealerships are middlemen between you and the bank, meaning they usually have a contract with the original loan agency to have a cut of every loan they dole out from their dealership. To avoid dealer markup, go straight to the loaning agency you wish to work with beforehand.

Another thing to keep in mind is considering putting some form of money down when dealing with the lending institution. The more financial risk you take on personally, the more willing they are to not simply give you a loan, but to give you a better interest rate.

Like when finding your dream RV, I encourage you to shop around a bit first. Make a few appointments with different banks to familiarize yourself with the terms, and use online tools to compare terms to figure out the best deal for your situation.

***

Know Your Credit Score

Also, just like a car loan, your credit score will be taken into consideration when obtaining a loan, as well as with the interest rate of the loan. Make sure to be familiar with yours before going in. And, just like a car, the original ticket price does not include things such as taxes, fees, and additional add-ons.

Your credit history is also checked when applying for an RV loan, so not only does your credit score come into play, but so does your payment history and any other debt you currently have. But rest assured: even those with a lower credit score can still get a loan for an RV if they go through the dealership, just be ready for a markup and a higher interest rate overall.

If it is possible, try to pay as much up front as possible. New RVs depreciate in value as much as 30% when someone drives it off the lot, so you will always owe significantly more on it than it is worth. But, if you pay some up front, like a down payment on a car, then you can avoid the type of heartache that comes with totaling an RV and not getting enough back from the insurance company to pay off the loan.

***

Mistakes to Avoid When Getting a Loan

You already learned that you need to be willing to negotiate the purchase price down. Any dollar you are not paying, you don't have to borrow! And you also know you need to know your credit score before obtaining a loan.

These are already two things you are going to do right!

To put yourself in the best possible position, here are some mistakes to avoid when trying to get a loan for your dream RV:

- **Not Shopping Around**: when you are researching loans, use the same strategy that I recommended for finding your dream motorhome. First get informed about your options, and only then pick the one that is most favorable for your situation. Visit a couple of banks, do your online research. Perhaps you already have an outstanding loan, and you can bundle it with a second loan at a discount, if you stick with the same provider?
- **Getting a Higher Loan Than You Can Afford**: before you get a loan, calculate what your income and expenses are going to be. You do not want to default on your loan payments, as this may trigger a clause in your contract that will increase your interest. When calculating your budget, do not only take day-to-day expenses like gas and groceries into account. Also factor in costs for maintenance, insurance, etc. When you are done, you may be surprised to see how little money is left that can be used to pay off the loan.
- **Getting a Loan That Exceeds the Future Sale Price of Your RV**: as we just covered, new RVs depreciate in value as much as 30% as soon as you take it around for its first spin. Never take out a loan for more than the future sale price. It would be best to make a big down payment when you buy the RV. And consider starting small. By buying a small RV, and selling or trading it in later on, you may be able to move your way up the RV ladder at a relatively low

risk.

***

Preparing to purchase an RV, whether new or used, is an experience that requires preparation as well as patience. And how you are going to finance such a purchase is one of the most important things you will need to figure out. By applying the advice above, and doing your own research, you will have a solid foundation for finding the best possible way to finance your future motorhome.

Once the preparation, testing, and inspections have eventually led to the purchase of your beautiful recreational vehicle, it is time to prepare for your new living situation. Let's look into that now!

5. Preparing For RV Living

"There are no secrets to success. It is the result of preparation, hard work, and learning from failure."

Colin Powell

<u>Key Takeaway</u>: *The biggest obstacle you will tackle when preparing for RV living is choosing a state to domicile in. After that, everything else falls into place. Since you no longer have a physical address, go digital as much as possible. If necessary, use the address of your current campsite or local post office to receive regular mail or packages. You may need to find a workaround when it comes to voting, medical care, and jury duty. Use common sense here, and take it one step at a time. Keep in mind that these are small challenges when seen in the bigger perspective of living a life on the road!*

Getting ready for living in an RV full-time means setting a lot of moving parts in motion. Arranging things like voting, mail, bills, and taxes are usually filled with many different questions with no coherent source to find all of this knowledge.

We are here to change that.

***

Choosing a Domicile State

The very first step is deciding where you want to be from. When living a nomadic lifestyle such as this, picking a domicile state is essential. Once you have a legal permanent address, everything falls into place fairly easily. The great thing about living this type of lifestyle is the fact that you can actually choose which state to "reside" in. For one, this greatly impacts your taxes. But, being a resident somewhere and being domiciled are two different things: a residence means you are physically living in a specific location, but having a domicile means you live within a state's locality and have intent to take up residency there.

"Bodily presence" is a term thrown around quite a bit in state laws, and every state defines this term differently. But, one thing to take into consideration is whether or not you are earning an income. If you are, then states that do not have state income tax are usually most appealing. However, we will make this easy: of the states that do not have state income tax, South Dakota, Texas, and Florida are the most popular choices for people living a nomadic lifestyle because of the lack of state income tax as well as their overly-flexible definition of "resident."

However, there are other things to take into consideration when choosing a state to domicile in:

- Insurance rates
- Sales tax rates
- Vehicle registration fees and requirements
- Taxation on retirement proceeds and non-earned income (which is very important if you are living this

sort of lifestyle off a 401-k, pension, Social Security, etc.)
- Property taxes
- Homeschooling laws (if you are living this lifestyle with children)
- And even the time that is required of you to live within the state

Where you wish to concentrate your state of domicile will depend on which of the above influences your lifestyle the most. But, two more important factors to consider when choosing a state of domicile are (i) your driver's license and tag renewal requirements – like whether you have to do it in person or not –, and (ii) jury duty obligations.

Yes, it can be a complex decision with researching and picking a state of domicile, but once you do, everything else easily falls into place.

The key to establishing intent for domicile is using that same address for everything:

- Insurance
- Vehicle registration
- Identification
- Taxes
  Voting
- Bank and credit card statements
- Bills, and
- Anything else that requires an address

The more "intent" you establish, the more rock-hard your "intent to settle" is, should it ever be called into question. Doing this allows you to cut ties with any other state you – or anyone else you live with – might have ties to, further proving your intent to settle.

However, establishing domicile status in a state does have its limits. If your nomadic life is going to come with living long enough in one state to establish residency anyway, then go ahead and make that your state of domicile. The reason why is that if your residency is ever called into question, and you are in a state that is more aggressive with taxes, they could potentially slap you with intent to evade statewide taxes as well as other fines that come with not registering your vehicle in a state you "obviously reside in."

***

How to Get a Permanent Address

Once you pick a state of domicile, it is time to get a permanent address. No, you cannot use a P.O. box as your primary address. One of the tactics is using a family member or friend's physical address. If you take this route, however, make sure it is someone you trust who is looking out for all of those important documents, such as:

- Jury summons
- Legal documents, and
- Tax notifications

Then, you need to set up with them how you will pick up that mail from them regularly (will they be holding it, trashing it, forwarding it to you somehow?). Another thing to consider is how stable their housing situation is. Why? Because if they move, you move.

However, in many states that are popular for nomadic travelers establishing domiciles, they have services that are specifically set up to support these types of issues. This service "gives" you a "permanent address" that can be legally used on everything:

- Bills
- Banking
- Voting
- Insurance
- IDs
- And everything else that needs proof of address.

Many of these services can also accept packages on your behalf and hold it for you, and some will even scan your mail electronically and forward it to you as they obtain it. There are fees with these services, but most of them charge under $10 a month for a basic package. Establishing one is very easy, with the process being only a simple sign-and-notarize process for some forms, and some power of attorney sheets if you want them to handle your vehicle registrations as well.

A point of warning, however: there are requirements by the Patriot Act to have an actual residential address on file for these types of accounts. This means that mail forwarding from a P.O. box or another service like this in another state is not acceptable. You are legally allowed to use a "next of kin" address in a different state, but do not try to explain your situation. This could call into question your domicile state, which then requires a whole lot of proof in terms of the residency of your forwarding address as well as your domicile intent in the state you have established.

***

Set up Electronic Deliveries

Once you have a state of domicile and a legal address to use, the easiest way to go about doing bills is going to be to convert them all to electronic deliveries. This will reduce the amount of overall mail you will have to be responsible for picking up, and it will make paying them easier. Why? Because online statements come with online links to pay online. Then, unsubscribe from all of those paper mailing lists and see if they have electronic ones. Just understand that snail mail is going to take some time before it catches up to your transitioning, and you will accumulate mail for a little while.

But, keeping track of things that will always come in the mail is necessary: know when your renewals for insurance policies happen and schedule a trip to get your mail. Know when your renewal tags will show up in the mail and prepare a trip to obtain them. Be proactive in these specific dates and times and get them down on a calendar that can easily remind you of the date, whether it is a hanging calendar or one on your phone.

***

Set up a Digital Signature

Many things, such as setting up voting and insurance, requires documents to be signed. But, it is not always practical to show up in person. Therefore, having a program that enables the electronic signature of documents is very important. Many official documents accept a digital signature, which means you could potentially eliminate paper mail even further than you already have at this point. This also comes in handy with contracts, selling big ticket items (such as cars), and handling insurance matters and issues.

For those that absolutely need to be filled out by hand, have a printer ready. These may be found at the campsite or post office, and if not, find a print shop in a town close by. Then, it is simply a matter of using an application on your phone, such as CamScanner, to take a picture of the document, scan it, enhance it, and shoot it back to the desired recipient via email.

***

Use the Campsite Address

There will still be times where you need a physical address to receive regular mail. Like when you order a package from Amazon.

Besides depending on local friends and family to receive your mail for you, another way to receive mail while being on the road legitimately is to use your current location at a campsite. Many campgrounds are happy to let you use their address for your mail, so long as you make your name and unit number on the campground clear to the person sending you the mail in the first place. There are some campgrounds that even service packaged deliveries to mailboxes that have the unit numbers on the grounds attached to them. Utilize the service if it is available!

***

Use the Local Post Office Address

One more way to receive mail or packages in a town you are residing in for a while is with general delivery. Basically, you can send your mail and packages to the town post office without having a P.O. box, and you can then pick it up as they are holding it behind the counter. They will hold all mail and packages up to 30 days, and it only takes your photo ID to claim everything.

A little trick? When ordering packages online, there is a way to have them delivered via general delivery: when you are filling out the shipping information and entering your billing address, click the button that says the delivery address is different from the billing one, then enter "PO BOX General Delivery" in the main address box. This forces many online retailers to default to a USPS delivery to the city and zip code specified.

***

Voting

In regards to voting, your legal domicile address is now what is used when you register to vote. Then, since you probably won't be showing up in person, make arrangements to have an absentee ballot sent out to you within plenty of time before the election date so you can fill it out and get it back in. It's as simple as that!

***

Medical Care

In terms of doctor's appointments and medical care, many cities have free clinics and medical centers that operate on a sliding scale, and some of these places simply provide the care at no cost to you. If your health insurance does not cover urgent cares and things of the sort in the state you are visiting, take advantage of these services.

Then, in terms of keeping your health records up to date, simply ask the doctor for an official copy of everything that was done. You can keep your own up to date healthcare records this way. The key to medical records is to keep them organized and readily available, whether you keep paper copies or electronic ones.

However, if you are over the age of 65 and on Medicare, then never fear: Medicare offers you benefits wherever you go, unless you are traveling outside of the U.S. If you are, purchase traveler's health insurance coverage to give you coverage just for these times.

Also, if you have past military service in your history and any service-related health conditions, you can acquire medical care via the Veterans Administration. While the coverage is determined by the length of time you served and your current annual income, it covers you anywhere you go as well.

If worrying about medications is an issue, then fret not: many medications with prescriptions can be ordered and delivered in the mail in 90-day supplies, and many pharmacies have nationwide servers so you can order your prescriptions from any pharmacy around the nation, so long as you use the same one.

***

Jury Duty

Another point of frustration for some full-time RV travelers is the civic duty of yourself as an American. Simply put: jury duty.

Some states are more forgiving of circumstances, and some are not. For those that are, simply explaining to them that you are out of town for a family outing suffices. For some courts, they will require you to reschedule once you are back in town, which makes this a hassle seeing as the point of traveling is to never be "back in town." For those types of courts, sometimes traveling back is the only way to go. This is something that needs to be worked into your savings budget: either a plane ticket back to your state of domicile to attend the jury duty gathering, or the gas money to take either the RV as a whole or the toad vehicle (the second vehicle many RV travelers haul behind their RVs), so the person being called into question for jury duty can make it back.

It is not a perfect plan, but attending jury duty in your state of domicile further cements your intent to settle, which will not bring your domicile status into question.

***

The hardest thing you will do, by far, is decide and establish your state of domicile. But once you do, many other moving parts fall into place simply by having a legal permanent address. There are downsides, like jury duty, that are sure to pop up along the way, but having a legal permanent address will help with many different billing and official matters in the long run.

But, this is not the only thing to reign in when choosing the nomadic life of living in an RV. The other big issue for you and your family is going to be your budget. How much do you need per month in order to be confident that you can pack your bags, toss them into the back of your new motorhome and hit the road?

6. How To Budget For The Road

*"I've been flying down the road
And I've been starving to be alone
And independent from the scene that I've known"*

Albuquerque – Neil Young

Key Takeaway: *A budget is the biggest stressor for anyone on the road. Start with a budget of $1,000/month and assess whether this would be enough. It all depends on what is coming in and going out. If you can find ways to save money and cut costs, you will be able to lower your monthly budget. And that difference really adds up over the year. The most popular budgets still have full-time RV travelers working while on the road. If you are willing to stay in one location for a longer period of time, you could save up some money doing a seasonal job, working in a restaurant, or maybe even working at the campsite. An even better solution would be to find a way to make money online, as this will truly make you location independent.*

So many people believe that a lavish fund of money is necessary to travel full-time and live this type of lifestyle. However, there are many people who travel and save for their necessities off simply $600 a month! Many of the tactics involved include putting back money and saving.

Many people who sit stationary in houses do not have the money to dole out of their checking account when car repairs are necessary. Usually, they pull that money from their savings account which they have been building for a few months.

The same concept applies when you are on the road.

***

Budget: Where to Start?

A good number to start with is a budget of $1,000 per month.

If you take the idea of $1,000 a month and break it down, a possible savings and split of money can look something like this:

- $50 in a savings account for vehicle maintenance and repair
- $200 for food
- $100 for vehicle insurance
- $50 for cell phone and internet access
- $250 for gas
- $25 for miscellaneous items
- $25 for entertainment, and
  $300 for on-road costs (such as nightly fees for campsites)

$50 in a savings account for vehicle maintenance and repair, $200 for food, $100 for vehicle insurance, $50 for cell phone and internet access, $250 for gas, $25 for miscellaneous items, and $25 for entertainment, and then $300 for on-road costs (such as nightly fees for campsites).

While the budget for food does not afford eating out every single night, it does afford you to eat well if you cook for yourself. The gas is also a bit low considering today's gas prices, but this simply means docking longer at campsites and possibly choosing campsites that allow you to dock for free in exchange for doing work around the campsite.

***

How to Save Money

Of course, there are many people who live off more than $1,000 a month while traveling, and then there are a lot who live off less. Those who live off less live a very sparse lifestyle, but the above rough outline shows you that the RV lifestyle can be done on as little as $1,000 a month. But, before any traveling scenario is taken on, making sure to have an accurate budget is necessary. And, if costs are an issue, there are always ways to cut them.

There are many different ways to save money. Here are some examples:

- Using smartphone apps that will be discussed later to chart out routes with the lowest gas prices
- Boondocking (parking overnight somewhere for free)
- Travel during off-peak driving hours so you do not waste gas sitting in traffic
- Regularly cleaning out the air filters in your RV

- Docking at campsites that offer free docking fees in exchange for voluntary work around the campsite, and
- Using surge protectors to keep your electronics safe

Many people who begin the lifestyle of living full-time in an RV can simply take the rent or mortgage money they were paying and transfer it over to the RV payment they now have. If you can purchase an RV with all cash, wonderful. However, many people cannot, so make sure the payment for the RV is worked into your monthly budget.

One way to offset some costs is to have a massive yard sale if you are choosing to live full-time out of your RV. This can help you downsize a lot of unnecessary materials and make a little side cash in order to get you started on your first official trip.

A savings account is crucial for this type of lifestyle. An RV will require regular maintenance, and having that account will help to make sure your RV will be well taken care of, without throwing off your monthly budget when something eventually happens.

Many people simply take the money they were using on utility bills and begin putting that in their savings account. However, if you are looking to cut your cost of living, then take the amount of money you were using to pay bills, cut it in half, and put half of it back into that savings account.

When creating a budget, all areas of your lifestyle need to be taken into consideration:

- Groceries

- Gas
- Insurance
- Maintenance fees for your vehicle(s)
- Rent/mortgage, if you have another actual place of residence
- Subscription services (phone and internet are the big ones)
- Medical costs
- Prescriptions
- A regular deposit into a savings account
- Campsite fees, and
- Miscellaneous fees (entertainment, cleaning products, water softeners, clothes, feminine products, band-aids, etc.)

With regard to medical expenses, draw up an average of what your medical costs during the year look like, divide it by 12, and put that amount of money back into your savings account. This will help cushion medical issues that inevitably pop up with yourself and those you are residing with. If you have a pet, the same advice applies.

All of the above need a place in your budget. And remember, when in doubt, overestimate. It is better to have money left over then get on the road and not have enough.

***

Finding a Job on the Road

Another major question that comes into play is whether or not you will work on the road. Some people take up full-time residence in their RV later in life when their pension and Social Security are their forms of payment, and that is fine. However, others take up this lifestyle early on in life, and working on the road can become a confusing topic.

For some people, working seasonally gets them by. They spend their allotted money from their savings during the year, then stop somewhere nice for a season and pick up a job working for $7 or $8 an hour. They split their paychecks between their savings account and their daily needs until they have refueled their savings account back to where they need it to be for the coming months. Then they get back on the road once more and continue on with their journey. The key thing here is to keep up your resume and make sure to have solid references so you can continue to take on seasonal jobs.

Some people save costs simply by staying in one area for long periods of time. Many people stay in an area for three or four months at a time because they enjoy the culture or scenery, and while they are there they find a part-time job washing dishes in a restaurant or working part-time in a diner. This then provides them with money they need to sustain themselves while they are there without dipping into their savings account. They take the extra money they are not spending and put it back into their savings accounts to build it up for their next trek across the country.

If none of the above options are palatable to you in terms of making money on the road to facilitate the above basic budget breakdown, then there are many other options available to you to work while you travel:

- You can work at one of your campsites as a campground host, and some places offer free docking fees for those that do this type of thing
- You could make crafts and sell them places
- You could also offer handyman services or side-job construction type of work (such as painting)
- And you could even offer up services you were offering when you were dwelling in a home, such as animal grooming services or things like website design.

However, there are just as many ways to make money online as there are offline.

***

Finding an Online Source of Income

What would fit your new RV lifestyle even better is if you are able to find a way to make money online. More and more people are swapping their 9-to-5 job for a life as a so-called digital nomad. With digital devices becoming more sophisticated every year, and fast internet speeds being omnipresent across the country, NOW is an excellent time to learn how to make money online, so you can really become location independent.

I can only scratch the surface here, as an entire book could be written about every single way that you could make money online. With all these methods, keep in mind that none of these are a get-rich-quick scheme. Just because you are creating a business online does not mean it is easy. But if you would rather work hard typing away behind your computer than working hard doing a seasonal job in the fields, consider yourself lucky that you are living in the digital age. Just 15 years ago, you would not have the opportunity to choose between the two.

Here are some ways in which you can make money online.

***

Blogging

It is really easy these days to get your blog up and running quickly. You don't need to be a coding expert. Just pick a Wordpress template, or use an even more visual site like Squarespace.

If you are considering starting a blog to make money, you need to decide beforehand if you are willing to put in the necessary time to grow it. The most important thing with blogging is...blogging! You need to post regularly, at least once a week. Make sure you pick a niche and decide who your target audience is going to be. You cannot please everyone. Instead, pick a specific niche and really cater to your target audience. For example, the blog CheapRVLiving.com targets people that are into living the RV lifestyle on a budget. A great idea!

To make money of blogging you will first need to establish a reader base, and that takes time. In order to attract more readers, educate yourself on 'search engine optimization' (SEO) and use a plugin like Yoast to make your posts show up in Google for relevant keywords.

Include a few affiliate links in your posts, but always keep in mind that content is king. People have a very developed 'BS radar' these days. So if you are only blogging for money and do not really care about your content, you are probably going to shoot yourself in the foot. In that case, you may be better off choosing an alternative method to make money online.

***

Selling on Amazon

Amazon is the leading e-commerce store in the United States. It generated 136 billion U.S. dollars in 2016 net sales and has over 300 million active customer accounts worldwide. But did you know Amazon allows third parties to sell on their platform too? You could sell on Amazon!

The most popular format is called Fulfillment By Amazon, or FBA. Basically what this means is that, after you have sourced a private label product and sent the inventory to Amazon's warehouses, Amazon will fulfill a customer's order of your product. For a small fee, they take care of the payment, shipping and potential returns.

This requires an initial investment upfront, because you will need to buy inventory first. But once you have everything set up, and your product is selling, all you will need to do is making sure you don't run out of inventory! Because your products are stocked in Amazon's warehouses instead of in your garage, FBA is a great way of making money online while being on the road!

***

Drop shipping

Another way of selling physical products is drop shipping. There are similarities with Amazon FBA, but the main difference is that with drop shipping you are selling someone else's branded product, not your own. This will reduce your margins, so you will need to look into selling more expensive items. The flipside though is that you are not purchasing any inventory upfront. Instead, you find local wholesale suppliers and make yourself the middleman between them and the customer.

The process is basically as follows:

- Choose a profitable product to sell
- Contact suppliers
- Get approved by these suppliers
- Create a web shop (this can be your own website, an Amazon listing, or both)
- Drive traffic to it
- Start selling!

Selling products through Amazon's fulfillment system is becoming more and more popular, because Amazon is just such a huge e-commerce site. But drop shipping is still a viable alternative if you want to sell physical products.

***

Teaching English

There are many ways in which you can now teach English online to eager students all around the world.

You can choose to start your own personal brand as an English teacher, and find students by giving away a ton of free value first. Think blog posts and Youtube videos.

But…you don't necessarily need to go out there and find your own students. Lots of online platforms are looking for native speakers to teach English to their students.

Here are some examples:

- Italki.com
- Verbalplanet.com
- iTutorGroup
- Nicetalk.com

Go check them out and see if teaching English online is something for you!

***

Freelancing

Do you have a specific skill set that you can monetize? Perhaps you are a good copywriter, or a graphic designer. Or maybe you speak multiple languages and can offer translation services? If so, this might be a great way of making some extra dollars on the road.

Even more so than with trying to land an online teaching job, there are a ton of websites that bring freelancers and potential clients together. Here are a few of the most popular websites:

- Upwork.com
- Fiverr.com

- Toptal.com
- Freelancer.com

There are also freelance websites that target specific niches, such as 99Designs.com for graphic design work. Do your own research and find the jobs that match your skills.

***

These are just a few ways in which you could make money online. And there are many more, such as creating video courses, starting a Youtube vlog, or affiliate marketing.

Whichever one you choose, do not spread yourself too thin. Understand that it takes time to build up traction for your blog or Amazon FBA product, or to build up a popular profile on Freelancing or English teaching websites.

Graham Bell once said: *"Concentrate all your thoughts upon the work at hand. The sun's rays do not burn until brought to a focus."*

Let this be your inspiration to focus on one thing. This will greatly increase your chances of knocking it out of the park!

7. Getting Along In An RV

"Sometimes I wonder how you put up with me. Then I remember, oh I put up with you, so we are even."

Popular Saying

<u>Key Takeaway</u>: *Just because you love and enjoy someone's company does not mean sharing an RV will always be fun and comfortable. Making sure everyone has their own space and responsibilities ensures peaceful traveling for everyone around the clock. Stick to your budget, communicate openly when things get heated, and you will get along great!*

Living in an RV full-time means residing in a much smaller space with those you care for. Whether it is your significant other or a pet, keeping the peace is just as much of a priority as saving money.

***

Make Sure Your RV Has Enough Room

The first thing to consider is whether or not the RV you are looking to purchase has enough room for everyone to live comfortably. If four people are attempting to maneuver in an RV cargo van, things are going to become miserable very quickly. This does not mean you have to go and spend hundreds of thousands of dollars on a massive bus, but it does mean that it is important that everyone has their own little space.

Remember: if you do not get along in a home, you will not get along in an RV!

***

Choose a Sturdy RV

Another thing to take into consideration is how sturdy the RV is. If traveling is the main goal for your decision to live in an RV full-time, then making sure it stands up to different weather changes is imperative. Being able to regulate the temperature well inside of the vehicle, no matter the conditions outside, will go a long way in making everyone comfortable.

***

Assign Roles

Make sure everyone has a role. For many, an RV needs at least a driver and a navigator. If the driver is attempting to do both, things become unsafe, but if someone is attempting to "backseat drive," things become tense.

Other roles in an RV are the "cleaner," who goes behind and makes sure things are latched for the road trip ahead and the "hunter," who makes sure none of the necessities are left behind (such as electronic chargers, outside chairs, etc.).

Dividing up the chores necessary every time you set up in a camp helps aid in getting space after traveling as well. If someone is responsible for the inward preparation, and someone else is responsible for the outward preparation, it creates automatic distance that can be exponentially important when traveling in a confined space with one another.

***

Respect Each Other's Storage Space

Yet another way to keep the peace is to respect each other's storage space. If one person begins to take over much of the storage space that is already limited within the RV, resentment can boil and arguments can happen. Divvy up the space accordingly and stick to it. It will help with things in the long run. One way to make sure no one overtakes any space is to not overpack. RV living is about downsizing. Knick knacks have no place (usually) and a massive and sprawling wardrobe will not work. If you are having trouble downsizing, then a monthly storage unit needs to be worked into your budget.

In an RV, everything has a place. Make sure to establish these places beforehand, and this will keep simple situations like "where is the boiling pot?" from escalating into intensely emotional situations.

***

Assign a Place For Your Pet

If you are traveling with pets, assigning them a place is imperative. The last thing you want is an animal darting in between your legs and underneath your feet as you are trying to maneuver (or drive) in an RV. Train them to sleep in that spot and be in that spot when the RV is moving. It will make a world of difference in how you live around your pet.

***

Avoid Clutter

Clutter is an RV's worst enemy and can lead to many arguments. Get into the habit of washing your dishes and storing them away whenever you are done eating. There are no barnyard sinks in RVs, so leaving dishes in the sink clutters a space very quickly. If you are someone who likes to toss their clothes around, then learn a new habit: put your clothes where they belong the moment they come off your body. An RV can seem much smaller very quickly once clutter begins to build.

***

Do Not Travel Too Much in One Day

Also, make sure not to travel too much in one day. RV living is about traveling, yes, but full-time RV living gives you all the time in the world to travel. This means traveling 10 hours in one day to go see that relative of yours is a thing of the past. Be leisurely. Take your time on the road. Never try to put more than 400 miles in a day on an RV. It will help you take in the scenery, as well as enjoy the traveling, rather than making that traveling a stressor.

***

Stick to Your Budget

A great way of making sure everyone gets along well is to prevent stressful situations.
One of the greatest tensions many experience when living on the road are the monetary fights.

That is why a whole chapter of this book is dedicated to calculating your budget! If you apply the lessons from that chapter, this stressor is eliminated from the high tensions already established with adjusting to living in a closer proximity to family and pets.

***

Communicate Openly

The most important way to keep the peace and diffuse highly emotional situations is to be communicative. Even if you are the type of person that needs space to breathe before tackling an emotional topic, you still need to be able to communicate clearly. Lack of communication between those dwelling in a small space like this will breed tensions and spawn raging arguments.

A book that may really help is 'The 5 Love Languages' by Gary Chapman. He argues that we can receive love in 5 different ways:

1. Acts of Service
2. Quality Time

3. Physical Touch
4. Receiving Gifts
5. Words of Affirmation

These are all love languages. Every person has a dominant love language. If that language is used when they are communicated with, they will feel loved the most. Now here is the key thing to take note of: Most partners do not share the same dominant love language!

And this is the cause of much friction. Because if we are not aware of the different love languages, we automatically project what works for us on our partner.

So your dominant love language may be 'Words of Affirmation', meaning you feel loved the most when your partner compliments you. But if your partner's dominant love language is 'Physical Touch', and you never hug her or hold her hand, there is going to be a problem: she is not going to feel loved. Even if you tell her "Honey you look stunning, I love you" 10 times per day!

If you are sharing an RV with others, you can really do a lot of damage control by learning about these love languages, and figuring out the preferred love language for you and your partner.

And if all else fails, lock yourself in the bathroom or take a walk to breathe, then emerge ready to talk.

***

There are many different ways to help establish peace in a full-time RV situation. Making sure you and your loved ones stay happy and on the same page means acknowledging, and accepting that everyone is different and needs their space and privacy. That space gives people a sense of independence and lays the groundwork for stress decompression on an individual level.

Luckily, there is one massive way to save money while on the road that can help eliminate budget stresses, and that has to do with where you stay overnight while on the road. It is called "boondocking," and it saves many travelers thousands of dollars over the course of an entire year.

8. Finding The Best Campgrounds, Paid Or Not

"The world is a book, and those who do not travel read only a page."

Saint Augustine

Key Takeaway: *The largest chunk of an RV budget, by far, are campgrounds and campsites. Boondocking is a way to save you thousands of dollars a year, but it is not for everyone. Even if you don't want to boondock, there are still ways to save on campsite fees.*

A main concern when living the RV lifestyle is where to park at night. Basically, you have two options:

- Boondocking
- A paid campsite

Paying a campsite needs no further explanation, but what is boondocking? We will look at that first, and then we will go over how you can use apps and various memberships to find a safe place to rest your head at night.

***

What is Boondocking

Boondocking is the phenomenon of utilizing nature itself, or a sanctioned parking lot, to dock for the night instead of paying a campsite. This has gone a long way in saving many individuals money because most of these places allow you to dock for free. The truth of the matter is that it is not always feasible to drive through the night (nor is it safe), and parking constantly at campgrounds can rack up a very serious bill. Therefore, many areas around the country, from free public lands to Walmart parking lots, all encourage the overnight docking of RVs.

But, how do you keep power? And water? Well, many people nowadays who live in an RV full-time are taking advantage of the tax credit that comes with installing solar panels and putting a few in specific areas of their RV. This gives them power no matter where they go and makes boondocking a lot easier. If you do not want to go full-on solar panel just yet, there are many portable solar panels that can be easily stored away when not necessary. However, you also have to keep that electricity usage efficient. Some ways to do that are not boondocking in areas that will require a constant use of the air conditioning or a heater, and switching the traditional bulbs in your RV to LED bulbs. Those will help save a lot of electricity in the long run.

With water, it is as simple as putting water into the outside reserve tank and using it. You know, like the water you use when you are traveling on the road. But, there is also the idea of water conservation. In order to boondock in luxury without having to worry about constantly refilling the water tank, there are things you can install and do to limit your overall water usage: install a low-flow shower head and a turn-off valve so you can shut the water off while you are lathering up. Low-flow faucet heads on your sink are also available, and if you want to invest in a solar shower (a small device that uses the sun streaming through your windows to heat up water in an insulated bag) for washing dishes and cleaning up, that will help conserve water as well.

But, how do you dump black water? And how do you know what areas will allow you to dock overnight for free?

Luckily, this is where smartphone apps come in handy.

***

Apps for Boondocking

You are very fortunate to live in today's world. Technology has advanced at an enormous speed these last decades. Did you know that by simply opening your browser on your smartphone you now have access to more information than Bill Clinton had when he was president?

Take a moment to let that sink in…

This is an amazing time to start considering living in an RV motorhome. There are so many online tools and apps at your disposal that I don't even know where to begin!

GasBuddy is a high-rated app that allows you to scour the nation for the lowest gas prices around. It works very well when planning your trips and trying to figure out how much gas will cost as you jump from state to state.

Some apps that will help you find boondocking stations are **US Public Lands** and the **Overnight Parking Walmart** app. Both of these will help you find free places to boondock for the evening to help plan your trip accordingly, and they will even provide addresses and phone numbers for people you can contact ahead of time if you have questions!

Yet another place that is friendly towards RV boondockers are truck stops, and there is an app called the **Truck Stops & Travel Plazas** that helps find truck stops that cater to RVs around the country.

However, the most useful app for people living in an RV full-time that boondock regularly to save money is the **RV Dumps** app. This is a sanitary dump locator for when your waste tanks are full and need to be dumped. It lists places with addresses all across the country, and also helps in planning trips. You can lay out a boondocking area that is near a dump, making everything seamless and worry-free for the road trip ahead.

One last app that many RVers use is **GPS Coordinates Finder**. Sometimes simply having your GPS coordinates can help whenever you get lost. And that is all this app does!

***

Campground Sites Memberships

If boondocking is not your thing, there are still ways to save money and have memberships at campground sites around the country.

For example, the **Good Sam RV Club** has a massive community that provides multiple services. They have a trip planning service that helps estimate fuel costs, aids in route planning, helps to locate other RV services (such as maintenancing) around your specific area, and helps locate viable rest stops along your route. Not only that, it provides a 10% discount upfront to any of their 1,600 camping sites in the U.S. and Canada.

But, their membership also includes things like emergency towing services, and can provide full RV coverage insurance for when you are traveling. It can help plug the holes in the insurance you already have, reducing your liability even more and keeping you worry-free throughout your journey.

Another club to join that can help reduce the costs of RV living is the **RV Golf Club**. The membership is $99/year, and this enables someone to park at several private golf courses and resorts for free. The locations have stunning views, no parking fee whatsoever, and this membership will help with discounts at the resorts and golf clubs if you are a golfer.

Harvest Hosts is a membership similar to RV Golf club, except it allows you to stay at parks of many listed wineries and specialty farms for free. Discounts on some of their products are available to those that have this membership, the docking is free, and the membership is only $40/year. The program currently has 470 sites, and it keeps on growing daily.

Escapees is another top-rated club, but it is more expensive than the others mentioned above. The membership fee is $39.95/year, and there is no enrollment fee. But, it does have other fees that rack up. This program offers shared discounts with other RV organizations that help save money on the road in the long run. It comes with benefits like 50% off at over 1,000 campgrounds across the nation, and the club itself has 19 five-star RV campgrounds where members can hook themselves up for $10-$15 dollars a night. The weekly rate for staying at a place like this is less than $100, which is beyond reasonable for long term stays, and those who want to dry camp (using their campsite without hooking up to their water and electricity) can park there for merely $5/night for up to 21 days!

***

It is very possible to keep campground sites and overnight fees from eating holes in your budget. These tactics alone can free up thousands of dollars a year, and can sometimes mean the difference between full-time RV living with a job versus without one. The above listed memberships are not the only ones available, but they are currently the top-rated ones in the nation. However, if boondocking is something you would want to do for simple overnight stays, then that is the biggest money-saver for many RV travelers.

Finding great campgrounds, no matter what you choose to do, is easy with the invention of tailored apps for smartphones. Use every single one of them to your benefit and you are sure to save a lot of money while you are traveling, while docking and camping in some of the nation's most beautiful terrain. Take advantage of the tax credits available to you to make boondocking a little more luxurious, and boondock offsite in public lands. Allow yourself to wake up to the sun rising over a sprawling lake as fish jump and thousands of birds serenade you in the background.

The views alone are priceless.

9. RV Resources

If you would like to learn more about RV Living, here are some great free resources to get you started.

***

RV Lifestyle Websites

- **Rvia.org**: Website of the Recreational Vehicle Industry Association (RVIA). Check out their calendar to find an RV show near you. Most shows are organized in spring, summer and fall.
- **CheapRVLiving.com**: Learn about how to live the RV lifestyle on the cheap.
- **TheRVGeeks.com**: Dedicated to educating you on RV maintenance, repair & travel tips. Also has an excellent Youtube channel with lots of educational videos.
- **Rvtravel.com**: Lots of info and advice for RVers here. Don't forget to subscribe to their great newsletter.
- **Technomadia.com**: Chris Dunphy, Cherie Ve Ard and their cat Kiki combine their expertise of technology with life on the road. Very inspirational if you are considering working online as a way to make money while traveling!
- **Doityourselfrv.com**: Great RV website, especially for those that consider themselves a DIY-expert.

***

RV Lifestyle Apps

- **GasBuddy**: Allows you to scour the nation for the lowest gas prices around.
- **US Public Lands**: Will help you find boondocking stations.
- **Overnight Parking Walmart**: Find Walmart locations where you are allowed to park your RV overnight.
- **Truck Stops & Travel Plazas**: Helps you find truck stops that cater to RVs.
- **RV Dumps**: Helps you locate places where you can dump the waste that has accumulated in your RV's waste tanks.
- **GPS Coordinates Finder**: Find your exact GPS coordinates. A lifesaver when you get lost!
- **Passport America**: Browse an international directory of 1900+ participating parks, campgrounds, and resorts.
- **CamScanner**: Take a photo of a document and make it look as if it was scanned. Perfect for when you need to submit a signed document.

***

Finding Campsites Websites

- **Roadnotes.com/product/walmart-rv-parking-directory/**: It is Walmart's official policy to allow RVers to park overnight on their parking lots. However, overnight parking is prohibited at approximately 800 Walmart stores (20% of all stores), mostly because of local laws and parking space availability. This PDF contains a list of all Walmart stores where it is not allowed to park your RV at night.

Is your local Walmart not in the list? Then you are good to go!
- **Campendium.com**: Database of over 21,000 different campgrounds, many of which are reviewed by other users. Also has a database of sanitary dump stations.
- **FreeCampsites.net**: A community-driven platform for sharing campgrounds and campsites. Great place to find free camping sites near you
- **Boondockerswelcome.com**: Connect with other RVers to hear tips and tricks about boondocking and life on the road on a budget.
- **Passportamerica.com**: Offers a 50% discount at their participating 1,900+ campgrounds in the U.S.

***

Making Money Online Websites

- **Wordpress.org**: Build your own website.
- **Squarespace.com**: Another platform to build your own website, more visual than Wordpress.
- **Amazon.com/fba**: Sell Private Label products on Amazon through Fulfillment By Amazon.
- **Italki.com**: Teach English online.
- **Verbalplanet.com**: Teach English online.
- **iTutorGroup**: Teach English online.
- **Nicetalk.com**: Teach English online.
- **Upwork.com**: Find work as a freelancer.
- **Fiverr.com**: Find work as a freelancer.
- **Toptal.com**: Find work as a freelancer.
- **Freelancer.com**: Find work as a freelancer.

***

Membership Websites

- **GoodSamClub.com**: Massive community that provides multiple services, including trip planning and emergency towing service.
- **RVGolfClub.com**: Enables you to park at several private golf courses and resorts for free.
- **HarvestHosts.com**: Similar to RV Golf club, except it allows you to stay at parks of many listed wineries and specialty farms for free.
- **Escapees.com**: Another top-rated club. Offers shared discounts with other RV organizations that help save money on the road in the long run.

***

Roadside Assistance Websites

- **Goodsamroadside.com**
- **Coach-Net.com**
- **Progressive.com**

Final Words

Thank you so much for taking the time to download this book *'RV Living: A Beginner's Guide To Turning Your Motorhome Dream Into Reality'*.

Now that you have read through it and digested the information at hand, you should have a thorough understanding of the basics that go into full-time RV living, how to create your own budget, how to choose which RV is right for you, and how to cope with the new lifestyle at hand. There are many moving parts that need to be jostled and changed when someone goes from living a stationary lifestyle to living a nomadic lifestyle, but that does not mean it cannot be navigated.

The key is research. Take it one step at a time and make sure you plan this out accordingly. Give yourself time to adjust as well as time to put everything together, and understand that everything comes with a learning curve.

Living in a recreational vehicle full-time can bring a fullness to life that stationary living sometimes cannot provide. For those wanting to live on a lower budget than they do now, RV living can provide exactly that. Enrich your life and travel. See the world around you. Meet new types of people and indulge in activities you never would have otherwise. That dream is possible with RV living.

I hope you have learned a lot about RV living, and feel comfortable – and excited – to make your dream of living in a motorhome come true!

BONUS CHAPTER: What Are Shipping Container Homes?

Below is the first chapter from one of my other books, *'Shipping Container Homes: Learn How To Build Your Own Shipping Container House and Live Your Dream!'*

Enjoy!

***

"We decided to build the home out of shipping containers because it uses less energy to re-purpose them than to recycle them (melt them down and remold the metal into something else). They are also really cool looking and add a fun industrial feel to the home. They are metal so we can use magnets all over the walls and they are almost indestructible. It's the first shipping container residence in our city... so we thought it would be cool to build the first one here in my hometown!"

Ryan Naylor, on why he decided to build a home out of shipping containers.

Key Takeaway: Shipping containers are sturdy, durable containers that are used to transport goods by sea all over the globe. Many of these shipping containers are only used once, and as a result can be bought for a low price. This, combined with the eco-friendly aspect of it, has sparked the *trend of shipping container homes: converting these big steel containers into living spaces. Shipping containers have been used to build living accommodations for students and even shopping malls. In this book you will learn how you can go about designing and building your own shipping container home.*

Purchasing or building a home is one of the biggest decisions you will make in your life, and possibly one of the most financially-taxing as well. There are many considerations you will need to put into account when selecting the type of house, how much space is necessary, design, materials, location, and other variables. It is a decision that has both short-term and long-term repercussions on your lifestyle, so you should equip yourself with as much knowledge and available options as possible.

In recent years, a trend that has grown in popularity among many home-buyers is the conversion of shipping containers into usable living spaces. How does that work?

***

Turning a Shipping Container Into a Home

Shipping containers are designed to carry all sorts of cargo by sea, to every corner of the world. They are made of steel, which makes them very sturdy. Also, they can withstand various elements of nature.

The majority of shipping containers in the world today come from China. It is estimated that there are around seventeen million of these containers around the world today.

Now check this: Many containers are only used once!

Did you know that? It blew my mind when I first heard it.

Often it is cheaper to let these one-trip containers gather dust at a shipping container graveyards close to shipping ports, than sending them back to their point of origin.

This, together with it being a cost-effective alternative to traditional housing options, has sparked the trend of converting these shipping containers into homes.

***

How Shipping Containers Are Used For Retail and Housing

Enterprising individuals have successfully converted these big steel containers into office or retail spaces worldwide.

For instance, in Le Havre, France, shipping containers were converted into 'Cité A Docks', a 100-apartment complex for students. Each unit is equipped with a bathroom, kitchen, and Wi-Fi access

Cité A Docks, Le Havre

Something similar has been done in Amsterdam, The Netherlands.

Keetwonen Project, Amsterdam

A lot of students struggle to find an apartment for a rent they can afford. To accommodate these students, the local government started the 'Keetwonen' project and had an impressive number of shipping container homes built. As a matter of fact, with 1,000 homes it is the world's largest container campus for students.

Meanwhile, in the United States, retailer Puma converted 24 shipping containers into a three-level, 11,000-square foot store and event venue. Dubbed as 'Puma City', the traveling store was completed in 2008 by the LOT-EK architectural firm, and has made stops in many cities.

Puma City

In a review of the Puma City concept store, Olivia Chen of Inhabit.com wrote: *"While the structure of the shipping containers is evident in the multiple frames created by the knocking down of the shipping containers' walls, the open and well-lit environment makes the industrial aesthetic seem almost intentional. Additionally, built-in details, such as the two decks located on the upper floors and recessed lighting, gives the store a greater sense a permanence and less like a prefabricated structure that can simply be folded up and moved."*

And finally, in Christchurch, New Zealand, a pop-up mall made from shipping containers was created after the 2011 earthquake in the city. Dubbed as 'Restart the Heart', the mall project made use of 60 shipping containers housing 27 shops.

Re:START mall, Christchurch

The Re:START mall project was initially envisioned to be a temporary retail space after the earthquake damaged much of the City Mall, but has become very popular among locals and tourists alike and it remains in business until today.

***

With the use of shipping containers becoming more and more mainstream for retail, office, and residences in many areas of the world, perhaps you are looking into this option as well.

Refurbishing shipping containers definitely offers a lot of flexibility and innovative design options for your home. Let's take a closer look at the advantages of converting these containers into residential units in the next chapter.

***

This is the end of this bonus chapter.

Want to continue reading?

Then get your copy of "Shipping Container Homes" at your favorite bookstore!

Did You Like This Book?

If you enjoyed this book, I would like to ask you for a favor. Would you be kind enough to share your thoughts and post a review of this book? Just a few sentences would already be really helpful.

Your voice is important for this book to reach as many people as possible.

The more reviews this book gets, the more people will be able to find it and also learn how they can fulfill their RV Living dream.

***

IF YOU DID NOT LIKE THIS BOOK, THEN PLEASE TELL ME!

You can email me at **feedback@semsoli.com**, to share with me what you did not like.

Perhaps I can change it.

A book does not have to be stagnant, in today's world. With feedback from readers like yourself, I can improve the book. So, you can impact the quality of this book, and I welcome your feedback. Help make this book better for everyone!

Thank you again for reading this book and good luck with applying everything you have learned!

I'm rooting for you...

About The Author

My name is Bill Oatfield, and I'm the author of this book on RV Living.

From a young age, I have always loved living life off the grid. What started small, with climbing trees and exploring the outdoors, developed into a profound interest in anything that would not confine me to the standard '9-5 get a mortgage' kinda lifestyle.

I wanted to experience real freedom. Without having to spend a fortune.

That's when I took a leap of faith, bought my first RV, and traveled across the country. It was not always easy, but I learned how to support myself on the way, and eventually created the lifestyle I always dreamed of.

Once I decided to settle down for a while, I built my own shipping container home. Did you know you can buy one at the fraction of the cost of a traditional home?

This lifestyle is not as difficult to reach as you may think. The most important thing is that you take action, one step at a time. I want to help you access that freedom, so you too can turn your dreams into reality!

By The Same Author

Notes

www.ingramcontent.com/pod-product-compliance
Lightning Source LLC
Chambersburg PA
CBHW052115110526
44592CB00013B/1617